First Facts®

PRO WRESTLING SUPERSTARS

THE **BIG SHOW** PRO WRESTLING SUPERSTAR

by Angie Peterson Kaelberer

Consultant: Mike Johnson, writer
PWInsider.com

CAPSTONE PRESS
a capstone imprint

First Facts are published by Capstone Press,
1710 Roe Crest Drive, North Mankato, Minnesota 56003
www.capstonepub.com

Library of Congress Cataloging-in-Publication Data
Kaelberer, Angie Peterson.
The Big Show / by Angie Peterson Kaelberer.
       pages cm. — (First facts. Pro wrestling superstars)
Includes bibliographical references and index.
Summary: "Profiles pro wrestler The Big Show, from his start in pro wrestling to his future endeavors"— Provided by publisher.
Audience: Age: 8.
Audience: Grade: K to Grade 3.
ISBN 978-1-4914-2058-4 (library binding) — ISBN 978-1-4914-2264-9 (ebook PDF)
1. Big Show, 1972– —Juvenile literature. 2. Wrestlers—United States—Biography—Juvenile literature. I. Title.
GV1196.B57K34 2015
796.812092—dc23
[B]
                                                      2014023793

Editorial Credits
Nikki Bruno Clapper, editor; Aruna Rangarajan, designer; Jo Miller, media researcher;
Katy LaVigne, production specialist

Photo Credits
Alamy: AF Archive, 18; Getty Images: Bongarts/Joern Pollex, 17, Ethan Miller, 14, WireImage/
Bob Levey, cover, John Barrett, 5, 6, 9, Stan Gelberg, 10; Landov: The Times-Picayune/Michael
Democker, 20; Michael Blair, 13

Design Elements
Shutterstock: i3alda, locote, optimarc

Printed in the United States of America in North Mankato, Minnesota.
092014   008482CGS15

TABLE OF CONTENTS

A BIG TITLE

It was November 1999. The Rock and Triple H were going head-to-head in Detroit, Michigan. They were competing in a Triple Threat match for the World Wrestling Entertainment (WWE) Championship. No one knew who the third **opponent** would be. Then Big Show walked into the ring. The huge wrestler grabbed the two men and slammed them to the mat. The match was on!

opponent—a person who competes against another person in a fight or contest

The Rock (left) and Triple H (right) faced each other many times in the ring.

FACT

Combined, Triple H and The Rock weigh 520 pounds (236 kilograms). At 425 pounds (193 kg), Big Show is only 95 pounds (43 kg) lighter than the other men together!

Big Show held the WWE championship title from November 1999 to January 2000. Then he lost it to Triple H.

Later in the match, three of Triple H's friends ran into the ring. Big Show fought them off. Then WWE owner Vince McMahon entered the ring. McMahon hit Triple H with the championship belt. Big Show finally pinned Triple H. The Big Show had tears in his eyes as he hugged the belt. At last he was the WWE Champion.

THE EARLY YEARS

Big Show's real name is Paul Wight. He was born February 8, 1972. Paul grew up in South Carolina. By age 14, he was 6 feet, 8 inches (203 centimeters) tall. Paul was still growing when he started college. He played basketball for Wichita State University in Kansas. Then he learned he had a disease called **acromegaly**. The treatment for it stopped Paul from growing. It also made him gain too much weight to play basketball.

acromegaly—a disease that happens when the body produces too much growth hormone

Big Show signs autographs for fans in his early years as a pro wrestler.

FACT

Classmates gave Paul the nickname Andre after huge pro wrestler Andre the Giant. Andre also had acromegaly.

In 1994 Hulk Hogan won the WCW Championship belt. He defeated Ric Flair.

FACT

At his largest, Hulk Hogan weighed about 300 pounds (136 kg)—125 pounds (57 kg) less than Big Show.

After college Paul met pro wrestler Hulk Hogan. Hogan told Paul his size would help make him a good pro wrestler. Paul started training to wrestle. In 1995 he joined World Championship Wrestling (WCW). Paul wrestled in WCW as The Giant. He won two World Heavyweight titles and four **tag team** titles.

tag team—when two wrestlers partner together against other teams

A FAN FAVORITE

Paul joined WWE in 1999. He wrestled as The Big Show, or just Big Show. He was a **heel** when he joined. But fans liked The Big Show and began to cheer for him. He became a **babyface**. Big Show teamed up with Undertaker to win his first title, the Tag Team Championship. In November 1999 he defeated The Rock for the WWE Championship. He held the title until January 2000.

heel—a wrestler who acts as a villain in the ring
babyface—a wrestler who acts as a hero in the ring

Undertaker (right) and Big Show were once teammates. Later they were rivals.

Big Show had size. Chris Jericho (right) had quickness. They were a powerful tag team.

FACT

The Big Show set a WWE record. He was the first to win championship titles for all three major U.S. pro wrestling companies.

In the early 2000s, Big Show won the WWE Championship again. He also teamed with Undertaker and Chris Jericho to win Tag Team Championships. But years of wrestling hurt his body. In late 2006 Big Show left WWE. He had to recover from injuries and get in better shape.

SIGNATURE MOVES

Two of Big Show's signature moves are called the chokeslam and the powerful KO Punch. Many of his fans know him for these moves.

signature move—the move for which a wrestler is best known

The Big Show returned to WWE in February 2008. He had lost more than 100 pounds (45 kg). In 2011 The Big Show won the World Heavyweight Championship in a Chairs Match. He beat Mark Henry. In 2012 Big Show won the Intercontinental Championship at WrestleMania. He won his second Heavyweight Championship in October of that year. This time he beat Sheamus.

Sheamus (left) was no match for Big Show, even after Big Show's dramatic weight loss. Here Big Show defeats Sheamus at a match in November 2012.

Big Show cheers on a group of kids in the movie *Knucklehead* .

The Big Show is known for his sense of humor. He sometimes does **impressions** of other wrestlers in the ring. His comedy skills helped him move into acting. In 2010 he starred in the movie *Knucklehead*. Big Show also appears in the movies *The Waterboy* and *MacGruber*. He had parts on TV shows such as *Royal Pains*, *Burn Notice*, and *Psych* as well.

impression—an imitation of the voice and actions of another person

THE FUTURE

The Big Show remains an important part of WWE's shows. In 2014 he had a big match with Brock Lesnar at the Royal Rumble. But Big Show won't wrestle forever. He may work as a WWE **announcer** or manager. He also hopes to keep acting. Whatever he chooses, the Big Show must go on.

announcer—a person who describes the action during a sports event

TIMELINE

1972 – Paul Wight Jr. is born on February 8 in Aiken, South Carolina.

1995 – Paul joins WCW as The Giant. He defeats Hulk Hogan for the WCW World Championship.

1999 – Paul joins WWE, wrestling as The Big Show. He wins his first WWE Championship.

2002 – The Big Show defeats Brock Lesnar to win the WWE Championship.

2006 – The Big Show defeats Rob Van Dam for the ECW Championship.

2010 – The Big Show teams with the Miz to win the Unified Tag Team Championship.

2011 – The Big Show defeats Mark Henry for the World Heavyweight Championship.

2012 – Big Show wins the Intercontinental Championship and the World Heavyweight titles.

GLOSSARY

acromegaly (a-krow-MEH-guh-lee)—a disease that happens when the body produces too much growth hormone

announcer (uh-NAUNS-uhr)—a person who describes the action during a sports event

babyface (BAY-bee-fayss)—a wrestler who acts as a hero in the ring

heel (HEEL)—a wrestler who acts as a villain in the ring

impression (im-PRESH-uhn)—an imitation of the voice and actions of another person

opponent (uh-POH-nuhnt)—a person who competes against another person in a fight or contest

signature move (SIG-nuh-chur MOOV)—the move for which a wrestler is best known

tag team (TAG TEEM)—when two wrestlers partner together against other teams

READ MORE

Nagelhout, Ryan. *The Big Show.* Superstars of Wrestling. New York: Gareth Stevens, 2013.

Price, Sean. *The Kids' Guide to Pro Wrestling.* Kids' Guides. Mankato, Minn.: Capstone Press, 2012.

Stone, Adam. *The Big Show.* Torque: Pro Wrestling Champions. Minneapolis: Bellwether Media, Inc., 2012.

Weil, Ann. *Pro Wrestling Greats.* Best of the Best. Mankato, Minn.: Capstone Publishers, 2012.

INTERNET SITES

FactHound offers a safe, fun way to find Internet sites related to this book. All of the sites on FactHound have been researched by our staff.

Here's all you do:

Visit *www.facthound.com*

Type in this code: 9781491420584

Super-cool stuff!

Check out projects, games and lots more at
www.capstonekids.com

23

INDEX